GETTING RESULTS THROUGH LEARNING

Patricia A. McLagan

TIPS FOR PARTICIPANTS
IN WORKSHOPS AND CONFERENCES

©1982 McLagan & Associates Products, Inc.
Revised 1985

ISBN 0-913147-20-6

McLagan & Associates Products, Inc.
St. Paul, Minnesota

You are about to spend a very
precious commodity — your time —
in a workshop or conference.

This book can help you
make the most of that time.

It's about getting results.

Not so long ago . . .

A major corporation held a conference:
- "to update management's understanding of the issues we face"
- "to broaden managers' knowledge of new techniques"
- "to motivate management to use more competitive methods."

The conference lasted four days and cost $600,000 — excluding the salaries of the executives who attended.

250 people
came
applauded
visited
watched and listened
(sometimes slept).

And left, remarking "That didn't apply to me — but it was good to see old friends."

At about the same time, 30 new supervisors from a government agency went through a Basic Supervision Course "to learn about motivation, planning, and organizing."

The course covered many basic supervisory theories.

The new supervisors
came (it was required)
applauded
listened, watched, and sometimes thought about other things
visited
solved some case problems.

And left, feeling that "I know more theory . . . but can I use it back on the job?"

That same week, hundreds of thousands of adults throughout the United States spent an hour or more in a course, conference, seminar or workshop — working for degrees, studying job-related and personal topics, qualifying for continuing education credits in their professions.

Millions of dollars per week, thousands of hours, untold quantities of time and money spent in training, education, and conference rooms instead of at home or on the job.

***With What Results* —**
for individuals, their families, their organizations, their professions?

It's often hard to tell.

We can speculate, however, that the **benefits** frequently could be greater. Better designs, more focused programs, tighter quality control and evaluation, and better teaching/presenting could all contribute to improved results for all.

But this book is not about any of these. Rather it focuses on better, more **expert participation.** For each of us, when we're in a participant/learner role, has the power and potential to **choose, customize,** and **manage** the results of that program **for us and our needs.**

The approaches and skills of participation are simple — but they are not often taught in our school systems, or consistently and thoughtfully practiced by very many adults when they attend programs.

The approaches and skills of participation are what this book is about.

It is for :

- the manager who is about to attend a management conference
- the new supervisor who has enrolled in a training course
- any adult who intends to spend personal or company dollars and time for a formal program to help him or her find knowledge, skills, and solutions that relate to important current or future needs and interests.

It is about **results** and **payoffs** — areas that each of us can manage, no matter what the situation.

A PLANNING OVERVIEW

Planning for Results

CHAPTER ONE

Handling Program Materials and Information

CHAPTER TWO

Learning

CHAPTER THREE

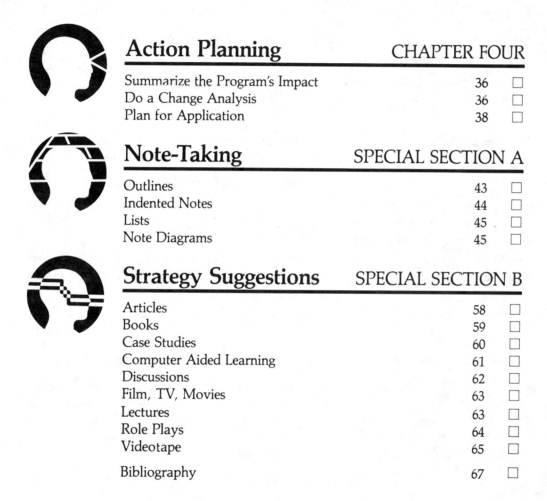

Action Planning
CHAPTER FOUR

Note-Taking
SPECIAL SECTION A

Strategy Suggestions
SPECIAL SECTION B

HOW TO USE THIS BOOK

A Note from the Author

There are some things you may want to know and do that will help you GET RESULTS from this book in the brief time you will probably be able to spend reading it:

Know what's in this book

This book contains:

BELIEFS

- that both participants and program leaders are responsible for getting RESULTS from workshops and conferences

- that effective program participation requires a greater variety of planning and learning skills than most people bring to these situations

- that participants can choose to accomplish any of a broad range of goals in a learning situation

A PERSPECTIVE

On adult learning that you can use as a framework for helping yourself (and others) manage learning situations. The implications go beyond workshops and conferences to virtually all situations where learning is a goal.

SPECIFIC TIPS FOR

- planning what you will get out of a workshop or conference

- handling course materials and information

- learning (remembering, building skills, changing priorities, spinning off creative ideas)

- bringing what you learn back to your job and your life

ACTION SUMMARIES

Each chapter of this book ends with a brief recap and with two QUESTIONS to consider during your reading and after each chapter:

- What do you want to remember from the chapter?

- What tips will you use (or modify and use)?

Many of the tips — while common sense — are not common practice. The ACTION SUMMARIES may help you examine the implications of the content at a level where you'll detect this discrepancy for yourself.

Set a time limit and develop a plan for reading this book.

There are 18,000 words in this book. At a 250 words per minute pace, that's 72 minutes of reading (if you read straight through). This, of course, is one option. Another is to read the "Planning Overview" on pages vi and vii. Then check off the sections that most interest you and either read them first or plan to read them more carefully than the other parts of this book. Whatever your strategy — let this book serve your needs.

Think for a few minutes about programs you attended in the past.

How satisfactory were the results from programs you attended in the past? Did they justify the time you spent and the other opportunities you passed up? What skills did you bring to the programs which helped you get results? What were your major frustrations?

The answers to these questions are an important personal backdrop for reading and using the ideas in this book.

Flip through the special sections on note-taking and learning strategies.

You may want to learn and use the new note-taking system presented in Special Section A. And you may want to refer to Special Section B for help in specific future situations. Tips there will help you get results from case studies, lectures, computer-aided learning, books and other sources.

Take this book with you to the programs you attend in the future. You'll find the tips take on new meaning from program to program.

In sum, *Getting Results through Learning: Tips for Participants in Workshops and Conferences* is about a manageable process. Some of the techniques, approaches, and assumptions presented may be new to you, others may be part of your current practice, and yet others may be in that "common sense but not common practice" category that is so blinding to action.

No matter where your current skills and practices fall, however, it's likely that this book can help you examine and refine them so that your results are more comprehensive and long-lasting.

Surely your gains will be worth a great deal more than the time it takes to read this book.

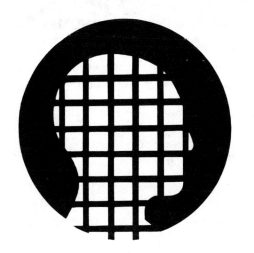

PLANNING FOR RESULTS

What impact can you expect from a program? What information will you most want to remember and use? What preparation makes sense? How will you participate?

A few minutes of planning before you attend a workshop or conference can help you begin to answer these questions and prepare for an effective experience.

Four quick steps will help you set up:

- Preview the program.

- Note potential benefits and results.

- Involve key people in your goal setting.

- Develop a program participation plan.

Preview the Program Content and Resources

A quick preview of content and resources can help you begin to identify a program's potential results for you. With this in mind, start your planning process by:

- reviewing the program announcement and making your own pre-program summary of the topics which will be addressed.

- scanning the lists of speakers, participants, and other resource people (including exhibitors) who will be available during your program stay.

Note Potential Benefits and Results

Now you're ready for the first step in matching the program to your needs — an important step that you'll refine throughout and after the program. For, although workshops and conferences are designed for group or mass distribution, program results and benefits are always individual issues. This means that unless you, as a participant, link the program to your needs and situations, your payoffs from a program are likely to be minimal.

This linkage best begins before the program starts and involves two activities:

- identifying current critical issues, problems, and concerns that you expect to be better able to address after the program

and

- determining which topics you want to remember the most about after the program.

You can expand or modify your key issues and topics throughout the program, but identifying these areas early will always have some significant immediate benefits for you — helping you:

- select sessions (if there are session choices)
- pay attention to relevant information
- ask questions
- influence discussions to address your concerns
- know when you'll want to apply memory techniques
- begin that all-important strategizing for real-world application.

These preliminary lists can also either help you increase your motivation to participate or help you recognize that the program may not be relevant enough to your needs to justify the time, energy and dollar tradeoffs involved.

 ## Involve Key People in Preliminary Goal Setting

If your program experience is effective, you may want to make changes which directly or indirectly affect your family, organization or others. You may, for example, bring back new time management methods that affect your secretary's workload or that change your delegation methods. You may learn new procedures for following up on sales calls that may have implications for your filing or record systems (and, therefore, impact others who use the system). You may learn new meeting management techniques that will affect how others must prepare for and participate in your meetings. You may want to explore new technical or organization structuring procedures that will affect other technical professionals or managers in your shop. Or, you may come out of a "career workshop" with plans that will affect your family.

The important pre-program implication here?

Since few changes (results) will occur in a vacuum, it may be useful before the program to review the upcoming program and discuss potential application areas with those people who:

- work closely with you and may have an interest in the topics or skills the program will address.

- control any major resources that you may want to tap into later (e.g., if you think you may want to experiment with some new manufacturing assembly techniques after the program, you may want to discuss assembly problems with the plant foreman before the program).

- will be affected in a major way if you change any of your practices (your boss, colleagues, subordinates, or family members, for example).

- have information that may make your goal setting more on target (your boss may have some useful insights into the political or dollar constraints on technological change ideas, for example).

It's an often proven fact that involvement in planning for change leads to greater commitment to implementing change later on. If you think you may come back from a program with change ideas that will affect others, get them involved in thinking about application areas and benefits before the program. Implementation later will be easier and more on target — and won't be a surprise to others.

 ## Develop a Program Participation Plan

Before you move into the program itself, then, it's a good idea to have a clear understanding of the topics to be addressed, the topics you are most interested in (and therefore will want to remember the most about), the people resources who will be available during the program, and the major personal and job issues you expect to troubleshoot throughout the program. It's a good idea also to have begun to "lobby" for expected change later on.

Then, based on these pre-program preparations, you'll be ready to develop a participation plan to:

- select sesions you'll attend

- identify people you will want to talk with during the program

- determine your preliminary results and goals for the program.

THE MAIN POINT IS

Although it's tempting to skip this phase and plunge right into the program itself, PLANNING is an important first step toward getting results from workshops and conferences you'll attend. Planning for results before the program can help you focus your energy more productively during and after the program. It need not take a great deal of time and will probably not be the final statement of your goals, but your planning should include:

- previewing program content and resources
- identifying potential benefits and results
- getting key people involved in preliminary goal setting
- developing a participation plan.

ACTION SUMMARY

What do you want to remember from this chapter?

_____

_____

_____

_____

_____

_____

_____

_____

What tips will you use (or modify and use)?

_____

_____

_____

_____

_____

_____

Your own summary is, as we'll stress later, one of the best ways to end a program (or chapter).

CHAPTER TWO

HANDLING PROGRAM MATERIALS & INFORMATION

TIPS

Concentrate and Manage Your Motivation
Take Focused Notes
Neutralize Bias: Your Own and the Program's
Vary Your Strategies

Information management is an increasingly critical concern for all of us, on the job, at home — and in formal learning situations. New technologies for information storage and retrieval are springing up everywhere to help us sort through and access larger quantities of data than we have personally handled in the past. Some of these technologies directly affect information presentations in workshops and conferences (computer simulations and games, audio and video technologies, computer-based research services, for example). The new technologies are changing the shape of the information we get in these situations. But few of these technologies can have as much impact on the results we get as the information handling techniques we ourselves use.

Let's look at the role information handling plays in the "getting results" process.

Information handling involves:

- making decisions about what to pay attention to in the programs you attend

- using techniques that help you bring the information you want to use into your immediate memory, notes and files.

Expert information management during the information processing stage can lead to higher quality (more relevant and streamlined) learning and application later. In fact, astute information managers use information handling methods that begin to translate information into action ideas and results even before program sessions have ended.

Several skills are especially important to speedy and effective information management in workshops and conferences. They include:

- concentrating and self-motivating

- note-taking

- detecting bias — in yourself and others

- using and varying strategies to fit the session formats which make up the program.

Concentrate and Manage Your Motivation

"I have a hard time keeping my mind on what's going on."

It's difficult to act on, remember, analyze, or argue with information you don't process in the first place. In fact, many statements of "I can't remember much of what happened" reflect attention and motivation lapses during a program rather than memory problems.

Being able to concentrate and self-motivate are key skills leading to better results later on. Briefly, let's look at three major types of concentration and self-motivation problems and what you might do about them when they arise. As with all the tips in the book, however, let these just be springboards to helping you more quickly recognize and create solutions for your own needs and concerns.

What to do when "This material is not immediately useful or interesting to me."

When your needs and the session content do not match, you have at least three major alternatives (which may not be equally possible for you to pursue in a given situation).

You can skip the irrelevant session.

You can increase your level of overt participation and influence by:

- asking questions
- raising a problem or situation to the speaker or group
- suggesting that discussion groups explore the practical implications of the content. ("Could we take ten minutes to discuss some of the ways people are considering using this information?")

You can increase your level of covert participation by:

- taking notes in a way which keeps your attention focused on the information. (See the section on note-taking for special tips.)
- trying to spin off as many creative ideas or action ideas as you can (even if they are only remotely related to the topic at hand).
- trying to identify the seven or so key points from the information. (Seven is the optimum number of points or categories most of us can easily remember on a topic at a specific point in time.)
- promising yourself a reward for getting something out of the session. ("If I get something out

of this and am reasonable attentive, I'll take an extra hour for socializing tonight.")

These are all simple suggestions — based on the following obvious, but often ignored, assumptions:

- concentration and needs-satisfaction go hand in hand
- some situations do not as directly relate to your needs as do others
- some of the responsibility for making programs needs-relevant (motivting) is yours as a participant
- there are many ways — some overt and some covert — to make situations more needs-relevant.

What to do when "There are too many distractions in this session."

Distractions are disruptive when they are more attention-demanding than the program. The task here is to make what you are learning more interesting than its competition (whether that competition is from noises, visual disturbances, or physical discomforts).

Some of these tips may help you when you are distracted:

- Use the tips for increasing your covert participa-

tion. They are geared to raising the interest value of the program information itself.

- Clear your work area of visual clutter. Visual "noise" can be very distracting. (Think about the impact a paper-loaded desk versus a clean one has on your concentration.)
- Ask that microphone volume, lights, temperature be adjusted to more comfortable levels. (I've seen many situations where people could not hear a speaker and yet said nothing!)
- Suggest that doors be closed, non-smoking rules be enforced or non-smoking areas be set up.

In short, directly control what you can (e.g., your own work area), speak up about problems that the facilitator or others can control, and activate more focused learning and information processing strategies to raise your interest to levels that can compete with those distractions over which you have no direct or indirect control.

What to do when, "I'm preoccupied, tense, or tired."

Anxieties, thoughts about issues and ideas not related to the program, and other personal distractions can cause major concentration problems, too. Again, it's important to pinpoint the source of the difficulties and then act to cope with or overcome them.

Two major sources of internal distraction are: (1) thought interference and (2) physical fatigue and tension.

Thought interference. From time to time, ideas which are neither related to the program's content nor to your needs may interfere with your learning effectiveness. These distractions include:

- remembering phone calls you must make

- thinking about things you must do when you get back home

- thinking about the difficulties and frustrations you may be experiencing in the program rather than doing something to remedy them.

Remember that you can consciously process only one thing at a time. Acknowledge, but get rid of, thought interference by:

- immediately writing down the phone calls and any thoughts you'll want to remember or refer to and expand on later. This will free you of distracting, but important, information and assure that you'll be able to act on it at a later time.

- replacing any thoughts about the frustrations or problems you may be facing in the program with positive ("here's what I'm going to gain") or problem solving ("here's what I have to do") thoughts. Negative self-thoughts are insidious limiters of personal exploration and change. Detecting and replacing self-defeating dialogues early is an essential concentration tool.

Physical Fatigue and Tension. These are predictable for most of us at certain times of the day and after lengthy periods of sitting or of routine activity. Deal with fatigue and tension by:

- periodically taking some deep breaths and systematically relaxing tense muscles. Tension may accumulate without your awareness. When it does, it depletes energy you could be using to help achieve your goals. Check for tension, and if it's there, relax it away. (Right now, are your shoulders relaxed? Your forehead? Ankles? Legs? Arms? Back?)

- suggesting a brief break when you feel you and the rest of the group may need one. Some speakers and group leaders have not yet learned that long periods of sitting are highly stressful to adults and can be counter-productive to learning.

Take Focused Notes

"Yes, I take notes. But they're not very systematic and I seldom review them after the program . . ."

Note-taking in programs is something most of us frequently do, but seldom in a way which fully uses the potential of this powerful information handling and learning tool.

Think about your notes and note-taking procedures for a moment. Do your notes:

- help you concentrate?

- help you identify and track key ideas?

- help you store ideas in a way that is easy to review later on?

- keep you focused on your action needs as well as on the program material?

- encourage you to spin off your own creative ideas while still participating in what's going on in the program?

The best note-taking methods can help you do all of these things.

Effective note-taking practices usually occur in three phases.

PHASE 1: PREPARATORY NOTES
Before a program session, identify and record the issues you expect to directly or indirectly address in the session.

PHASE 2: SESSION NOTES
During each session, use an appropriate mix of note-taking methods to record information which relates to your needs and to keep track of any creative or action ideas that occur to you.

PHASE 3: SUMMARY NOTES
After the session, recap the key points in a seven (or fewer) point summary. (Remember that "7" is the number of ideas that, for most of us, is most easily recalled.)

Notes can be an exceptionally valuable information-tracking and organizing tool — when they are planned, meaningfully categorized, and summarized for quick review and action later on. There are many types of note-taking systems which you can use — and many possible formats for organizing these notes.

The note systems described in the Special Section on Note-Taking can be powerful — and easy-to-use — aids to taking useful notes. Hopefully, you'll find them beneficial in the workshops and conferences you attend in the future.

 ## Neutralize Bias: Your Own and the Program's

Biases — yours and the program's — are important to detect and address, for they are the filters which determine what information you'll act on after the program.

Specifically, your biases (your interests, attitudes, values, beliefs, opinions, preferences) affect:

- your choices of sessions to attend, of information to concentrate on, of what you will learn and of what you will use

- your interpretations of how you hear and see what is happening in the program

- your evaluations of what you agree or disagree with, how positively you react to the program or sessions.

If you do not recognize and at least temporarily neutralize your biases, they may interfere with the unbiased participation that is so critical to learning and personal growth.

Ask yourself questions like:

- How interested am I in this topic? How important do I think it is?

- What are people in the program saying about the topic that I don't agree with — or think is not important? Am I missing something by not taking a fresh look?

- Objectively, what are the key points others are making — irrespective of their apparent value to me? (Wait until later to evaluate.)

But questions that help you zero in on your own biases are only the start. It's also important to detect and neutralize biases in the program.

Watch especially for bias in the information:

- How up-to-date is it?

- How broad or narrow is the range of viewpoints it presents?

- How well-supported are the conclusions?

- What is the ratio of fact to opinion?

Bias in how the information is presented:

- How compelling (or boring) is the presentation style?

- Are advantages and successes described, but not the disadvantages or failures?

Bias relative to the speaker or facilitator:

- What is the speaker's background?

- Is the leader a high status, "famous" person? Or not well-known?

- How attractive, articulate, persuasive is the leader?

In some situations, you may not be able to do more than be aware of the biases in a program. In others, you may be able to help broaden the issues addressed by asking questions and contributing other points of view.

In any event, your own and the program's biases are filters that affect the content and quality of the information that is your data base for results later on. Be aware of the biases that are present and neutralize them where necessary.

 # Vary Your Strategies

The "tips" you've read about so far are generally applicable to all types of program situations. Different formats and methods within programs and sessions, however, may call for unique strategies and combinations of techniques. (Strategies for handling information from lectures must differ from those you use in discussion, role plays, etc.) Only when your information handling strategies take the idiosyncrasies of each format into account can you manage each situation toward your own goals.

Formats change from program to program — and within programs and sessions. The formats used most frequently in workshops, courses, and conferences are:

- articles
- books
- case studies
- computer aided learning

- discussions
- films, TV, movies
- lectures
- role plays
- videotaping sessions.

You will find specific tips for each of these in the Special Section on Strategies (pages 57-66). Please consider each set of suggestions as a starting point for creating your own best strategies.

THE MAIN POINT IS

Clearly, what you do to handle information in any program depends on your needs — as well as on the content and format themselves. Perhaps you will want to be more systematic, to spend more time planning, using concentration aids, taking notes, detecting biases.

Whatever your strategy choices, the challenge remains the same:

How to manage the program and your immediate response to it so that you get what you need from each session.

How you handle information can have an immeasurable impact on what you'll learn — for you can only learn and use what you've allowed yourself to process.

ACTION SUMMARY

What do you want to remember from this chapter (in 7 or less points)?

_____

_____

_____

_____

_____

What tips will you use (or modify and use)?

_____

_____

_____

_____

_____

_____

LEARNING

Well. This may exaggerate the point — but just processing information does not assure learning. No matter how well you concentrate, how organized your notes, how needs-focused and bias-aware you are, how appropriate your strategies . . . learning (remembering, developing skills, changing priorities, spinning off creative ideas) will usually require strategies beyond information processing. And — each "learning result"

- Remembered Information

- Skills

- Changed Priorities

- Creative Ideas

involves different strategies to bring it about.

 ## Remember

When you want to remember facts, concepts, methods, ideas, it's not enough to just "process" the information. You must develop:

A Thinking Framework for Improving Memory.

Five steps are key to remembering.

SELECT
Select what you want to remember. Trying to remember everything is not an efficient use of your memory system and may create an overload which actually blocks the memory process.

ORGANIZE
Try to organize information on any topic into seven or fewer main points. When possible, you can decide your main points at the beginning of a session. Or you may develop them later — as you reflect on your experiences in each part of the program. "Seven" appears to be a magic memory number.

ASSOCIATE
Mentally file information using some of the same logic you would use to store a report in a paper or computer file. Categorize and cross-reference, in a word — ASSOCIATE ideas with each other — and consciously relate them to issues, situations, information and experiences that are already in your data and experience store. The Note Diagram method described on pages 45 to 55 graphically associates details to main points and can be an excellent filing and memory aid.

TRANSLATE
Translate the information into your own words.

After all, you'll use your own words to retrieve the information. Anything you've mentally filed using someone else's terminology may be difficult — or impossible — to find. Hedge against that situation by rewording what you know you'll want to remember later on and by using your own words in your notes.

REVIEW

Review what you want to remember. Review and summarize immediately after each program session, if you can. Completing an Executive Summary is a simple but powerful way to review. Then, review at the end of the program. The pay off? At least twice as much retained information than you'd remember without a review. (Think about that — a brief review can be as valuable in terms of results as hours of note-taking in a session.)

Obviously, remembering is a filing and retrieval process. It requires the same attention as developing and using an effective paper or computer-aided filing system. Certainly, the consequences of not using careful filing methods are the same. We all know how difficult it is to find papers and computerized data that have been misfiled, filed using terminology that isn't really ours, filed indiscriminately with unimportant data, or stacked up in a corner and not filed at all.

Yet, many of us make the very same filing mistakes when we try to "memorize."

The five memory strategies are simple but very effective ways to vastly improve MEMORY RESULTS from the workshops and conferences you'll attend. Set aside the very small amounts of reflection time that these steps require and you'll achieve benefits far beyond the payoffs that come from just "sitting through."

In short, when you choose REMEMBERING as a learning result, use these strategies:
- select
- organize
- associate
- translate
- review

 Develop Skills

Frequently, your goals extend beyond remembering to developing skills. There are five major types of skills which you may want as results from your program participation.

Physical Skills — like learning tennis, karate, and other skills requiring new levels of stamina, strength, and body coordination.

Technical/Mechanical Skills — like learning how to fix a computer, assemble equipment, trouble-shoot a machine.

Interpersonal Skills — like learning how to conduct a performance review, work effectively in a group, lead a discussion.

Intellectual Skills — like learning to write a poem, read more effectively, organize a speech, apply a concept or theory to a situation.

Self-management Skills — learning how to learn, manage stress, self-motivate.

You can master skills in each of these areas by using variations of five tips that are part of:

A Thinking Framework for Managing Skills Development.

The following steps can be the basis for your skills building strategy:

IDENTIFY SKILL STEPS

What steps are involved in the skill? In what sequence? When?

GET KNOWLEDGE

What do you need to know and understand in order to use the skill appropriately?

PRACTICE

What skill steps do you need to practice?
What skill steps do you need to watch others do?

DEVELOP SUPPORTIVE INTERNAL DIALOGUE

What do you usually say to yourself when you are in a situation requiring the skill?

What are you saying to yourself as you practice and initially use the new skill — or aspects of it?

How can you make your self-statements more supportive?*

GET FEEDBACK

At what stages in your skill development and skill use will you need to examine how well you're doing — either for support or for taking corrective action?

Who can provide that feedback? (Consider

---

*A supportive self-statement is one that expresses confidence in your ability to do what needs to be done ("I'm going to take this one step at a time and expect to see gradual improvement."), or that involves problem solving ("Well, that didn't work, next time I'll need to . . .").

A negative self-statement is one that predicts failure ("I'll never be as good as Pete."), discounts you and your ability to change ("I'm too old and set in my ways to be able to change how I work with people."), or sees setbacks as insurmountable ("Well, that didn't work, I quit.").

your own self-feedback as well as feedback from others.)

Successful skill development requires all five steps, but the emphasis you place on each of them depends on you as well as on the type of skill you want to develop. Obviously, your abilities, initial skill level, anxiety and confidence level vis-a-vis the skill, and the support you get from people around you will affect your learning success.

The emphasis you place on each of these steps also depends on whether you are learning or just refining the skill. For example, if the skill is new, it's important to pay careful attention to:

• the skill steps

• knowledge development

• practice

• building supportive initial dialogues (and recognizing and replacing any negative or self-defeating thoughts about your ability or potential success)

• getting feedback.

Clearly, the early stages of learning require patience, perseverance, and frequent feedback.

The more carefully you manage those early stages, though, the faster you'll move to higher levels of skill expertise where the skill is reasonable, self-supporting and doesn't require the conscious attention that was necessary early in the process.

Again, the learning strategies you'll use depend on many factors:

• you

• the type of skill you're working on

• your current expertise in the skill area

• the supportiveness of people in the workshop, seminar, course, or conference, and later, of the people around you as you routinize your skill.

And, the strategies in skill development are different from those you'd use for other learning results. Be aware of what they are, and when you choose DEVELOPING SKILLS as a learning result, consider using these strategies:

• identify skill steps

• get knowledge

• practice

• develop supportive internal dialogue

• get feedback.

Change Priorities

Workshops and conferences can also lead to changes in priorities. That is, you may change your values, biases, opinions, or beliefs in a way that alters:

- how you evaluate situations and alternatives in the future

- how you allocate your time

- how positively or negatively you feel about an issue or situation

- how supportive or resistant you will be when specific situations arise.

The following are examples of changed priorities:

- A manager leaves a management development program with a greater sense of the advantages of participative management practices. His entire belief system about how he as a manager should relate with his employees has changed. He may or may not have developed all the skills he needs to fully carry out a shift in his management practices, but he will evaluate and select action alternatives differently because of his program participation.

- A technical specialist leaves a course on new applications of electronics feeling less fearful about this new technology and more positive about its merits and her place in its implementation.

- A building superintendent leaves a conference on business architecture with a greater understanding of the problems physically handicapped people face in their workplace and of the legal requirements to accommodate their needs. He understands the importance of bringing his building into compliance and recognizes that some of his construction decisions in the future will be based on the needs of this special group of employees rather than on cost-effectiveness criteria.

- You leave this book with a new perspective on your role in workshops and conferences. The book has helped you want to spend time planning for and managing your results.

As you saw in Chapter 2 ("Handling Program Materials & Information"), values, attitudes, beliefs, biases, opinions, interests are all words that describe personal information filters. They affect:

- how you choose to spend your time
- how you interpret events
- what alternatives you favor in decision situations
- how you evaluate the usefulness of tips and strategies.

The point is, sometimes these evaluation criteria — these personal PRIORITIES — themselves need to be changed. You can become skillful at this by developing:

A Thinking Framework for Examining and Changing Priorities.

Managing your own priority change is tricky business, for in some cases it may require challenging some of your most important values and beliefs. For some people, this may always be a highly traumatic thing to do. All of us certainly have at least a few very sensitive values, beliefs, opinions that we reflexively protect and are reluctant to challenge and change — even when the evidence overwhelmingly favors change. (Look at our response to the energy situation in the U.S. Many people have found it difficult to replace old personal comfort, speed, convenience priorities with conservative, social responsibility priorities

— even though there is compelling evidence that our economic well-being depends on this priority shift.)

Priority change is sometimes, then, a key prerequisite to personal growth and even to survival (in a job, in a group, in virtually any role).

How can you manage it — when it's an appropriate learning result for you?

Consider the following steps:

RECOGNIZE WHEN PRIORITIES ARE THE CRITICAL LEARNING ISSUE

This is a crucial and difficult step — for we are often not conscious of the values, attitudes and biases we bring to workshops and conferences. One quick way to recognize when priorities are the critical learning issue is to ask yourself the following series of questions:

- What action does this session advocate?
- Do I do it already? If the answer is no, then . . .
- Do I understand what that action involves? (Do I have the knowledge I need?) If the answer is yes, then . . .
- Can I do it? (Do I have the skill?) If the answer is yes, then . . .
- Other actions must be higher priorities.

What is the Action?

This course on time management suggests I set objectives every day.

Do I do it already?

I don't set objectives every day . . .

Do I have the knowledge I need?

. . . But I do understand the theory of setting objectives.

Do I have the skill?

. . . and I can write clear objectives.

Other actions must be higher priorities!

Then, why don't I do it? . . .

COMPARE PRIORITIES

When a changed priority is a possible learning goal, spend some time clarifying your and the program's priorities. Comparing priorities, however, may require some inferences — *for often neither you nor the program leaders enter a session with priority change as a goal.*

Think for a minute about the following situation:

A MINI-CASE EXAMPLE

A new Customer Service Representative attends a Customer Service Workshop. He expects to learn:

• What major problems may occur with each of the products his department may be asked to service.

An explicit knowledge objective of the program.

• How to identify what the specific problems are.

• How to deal with irate customers.

Explicit skill objectives of the program.

What he does not realize — and what is not specifically stated as an objective — is that:

• It is important to take extra steps and time to find out how the customer feels and to help the customer leave with a positive attitude toward the company.

An implicit priority change objective of the program.

Up to now, the Customer Service Representative has been trying to run as many repair orders as possible through the system. Spending time building positive customer relations has been an intrusion and not a priority.

If the representative recognizes and compares these priority discrepancies, he'll be in a position to decide if a change is needed at the priorities level in addition to — or in place of — knowledge/skill changes.

Comparing priorities requires going beyond the explicit goals and content of a program. It involves asking — "What assumptions do I and the program leaders have about the best ways to spend time?" When there are differences, priority change is a potential learning result that you might have overlooked had you not made the comparison.

EXAMINE THE PROS & CONS OF PRIORITY CHANGE

Once you've compared your and the program's priorities, you can look at the pros and cons of keeping and changing your current values, interests, beliefs.

Ask yourself — visualize — "What if . . . ?"

- What if I involved more people in business decisions?

- What if I changed the way I take notes in a course?

- What if I tried to get better results?

- What if I really spent time helping customers work through their anger?

- What if I set aside time early in the morning to set objectives for the day?

- What if I were more deliberate in my program participation?

- What if I don't make any changes?

And also ask yourself what specific situations and actions in your work and life will be affected if you do make a priority (value) change.

- You've decided that you may give higher priority to energy conservation. What does this mean for your house heating and cooling? Your driving? Your work habits?

- You're beginning to see that it's important to provide more customer-sensitive service. What will you need to spend more time doing? What trade-offs will you make (e.g., plan to do paperwork early in the morning before customers arrive).

- You recognize that you'll get far more out of a conference if you spend time "planning for results." What will you need to do? When?

- You've decided to consider adopting a more participative management style. When will you encourage participation? What changes in how you conduct meetings, in how you delegate, in how you plan — will be required?

- You've decided to spend your first 15 minutes in the office setting goals for the day. How will your secretary be affected? How will you handle phone calls and other interruptions?

DECIDE PRIORITY SHIFTS

At this point you can make a tentative decision to develop a new management style, to use different criteria in making decisions, to reprioritize your time, to monitor and counteract old biases.

DEVELOP A PAYOFF LIST

Then, once you've decided to change your priorities, give yourself some motivational support. Think about as many advantages as you can for bringing the change about. Make a personal payoff list that focuses entirely on the benefits of change or that describes some special rewards you will give yourself as you make the change.

This payoff list is a self-persuasion strategy geared at changing your beliefs, self-statements, and visions of how you spend your time.

Workshops and conferences provide many opportunities for clarifying and modifying priorities. For many of us, however, this is an ignored —often resisted — learning result. But, why is this true?

I think it's partly because priority shifts are seldom directly addressed in programs (or elsewhere, for that matter). We are encouraged to pick up new knowledge or skills — but rarely to examine the assumptions that underlie them.

And priorities — reflecting our values, attitudes, beliefs, biases, interests — are often very visible expressions of us as individuals. Deliberately changing them (for example, becoming a more participative manager), may appear to confuse our own or others' views of who we are.

Yet, in truth, priority shifts occur for us all the time. At different stages in our lives we value different ways of spending our time — with our families, on the job, during vacations. Priority changes are part of the natural learning and development process throughout the lifespan. Managing priority changes effectively so that they occur at appropriate times (i.e., before problems occur that force us to reexamine them) is an important life skill. For your purposes here, though, it is also a skill that can make your program participation far more valuable for your own personal growth.

After all, programs are supposed to accelerate as well as aid the development process. Whether they do or not often depends on the attention we pay to this learning result.

When you choose NEW PRIORITIES as a learning result, use these strategies:

- recognize when priorities are the critical learning issue

- compare priorities — yours and the program's

- examine the pros and cons of priority change
- decide priority shifts
- develop a payoff list.

 # Generate Creative Ideas

Creativity is not often recognized as a learning result. Yet some of the most frequently occurring benefits from workshops and conferences are the spin-off ideas you "create" as you participate in these programs.

Sometimes creativity involves new *steps or procedures*.

A manager hears about problems in a developing country. She spins off a list of new steps she can take to help her manage her department more effectively.

Sometimes creativity involves *new products*.

A chemist watches a film on arctic water life. It triggers a formula for the new solvent he has been trying for months to develop.

Sometimes creativity involves new *names* for things, events, people.

A judo instructor attending a physiology class comes up with a new name for some protective equipment she has developed.

Sometimes creativity involves the development of *new theories*.

An economist participates in a conference panel on stock market cycles. He develops a new theory about stock buying behavior.

Creative ideas are natural and frequent results of program participation. This is partly because programs are non-routine events that offer a fresh environment for thinking about and solving problems — even when those problems do not directly relate to the program content.

The participant's task is to recognize and foster this learning result when it occurs by developing:

A Thinking Framework for Creativity in Workshops and Conferences.

Any program has creative potential. Your major task in realizing this learning result is to *let it happen*.

Three steps can help you do just that:

SET UP FOR CREATIVITY

Early in the program — and at the beginning of

each session, "prime" yourself for creativity by listing some of the problems or issues that you would most like to solve.

These need not be directly related to the program content.

SHIFT YOUR FOCUS TO THE PROGRAM CONTENT

Once you've "set up" for creativity, shift your attention away from the problems and issues you've listed. Concentrate, instead, on the program information. If you've "set up" carefully, your own needs will "incubate" and a free association between your needs and the program information will occur without your having to manage that process.

RECORD CREATIVE THOUGHTS

Finally, write down the creative ideas that occur to you — even if they seem absurd or trite. Sometimes strange thoughts and associations carry the seeds of valuable and powerful ideas and solutions. (Gravity was discovered because an apple fell on a man who was both curious about the rules governing motion and ready to use any experience as a learning base.) Make it a point to judge and evaluate at a later time.

Recording all creative ideas will help you:

- be more aware of your own creativity when it occurs
- tap into your creative rhythms (you'll probably notice that creativity levels vary predictably throughout a day)
- develop a base for spinning off more ideas later on
- remember the creative thoughts you generate during the program.

Creativity is an amazing human capability. Many of us have been encouraged to suppress it — especially in learning situations. (How many tests during your school years encouraged you to generate new names for things, new ideas, new procedures, or theories?) It's a major adult learning task to reintegrate this learning result. For most of us this means just "letting it happen."

Three simple steps can set the stage. When you choose CREATIVITY as a learning result, use these strategies:

- set up for creativity
- shift focus to the program content
- record creative thoughts.

Your own imagination will do the rest.

THE MAIN POINT IS

Learning is

- remembering
- developing skills
- changing priorities
- generating creative ideas.

It involves more than just information handling. Each type of learning result requires special and unique strategies. The payoff? A much larger and longer-lasting store of personal competence — competence that you hopefully will use after the program.

But, as you'll see in the next section, using what you've learned involves some simple but additional steps.

ACTION SUMMARY

What do you want to remember from this chapter (in seven or less points)?

_____

_____

_____

_____

_____

_____

_____

What tips will you use (or modify and use)?

_____

_____

_____

_____

_____

_____

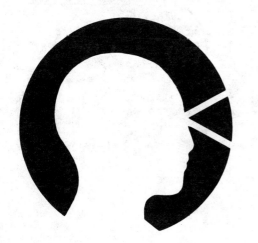

ACTION PLANNING

There's no doubt about it — using what you learn from a workshop or conference involves more than the steps we've covered so far — for you can:

- remember
- build skills
- change your priorities
- create ideas

and still not do or accomplish anything different after a program.

What Gets in the Way

Three major problems can prevent the use of what you've learned.

- Not developing the level of personal competence (knowledge, skills, priority, creativity) needed for accomplishing the changes you desire. This means it's important to be able to do what you need to do in order to make personal, group, or organizational change happen.

- Not considering the auxiliary changes that are necessary for successful change to occur. Most changes require other changes. A change in a personal habit usually requires "environmental" changes. *(I decide to eat only foods low in carbohydrates; therefore, I must also change my buying patterns. A change in management practices requires changes in how other people work. I become more participative; therefore, my employees and boss must be encouraged and helped to become more participative.)*

- Not allowing an appropriate time frame for change or for its impact. There is usually a time lag between the change goal and consistently successful action. *(I decide to change my public speaking style but must go through several improvement stages before I reach my goal. I decide to change the company's advertising image but find that commitments I made and ads I wrote months ago are programmed to run for the next three months. I decide to spend more time listening to customer complaints and less time filling out complaint analysis forms. But, it takes the Repairs Department four months to realize that although the forms are turned in later than usual, they are far more accurate and informative because I am taking more time with the customer.)*

Three tips should help you anticipate and deal with these problems so that you get the kind and breadth of results you need from workshops and conferences:

- summarize the program's impact

- do a change analysis
- plan for application.

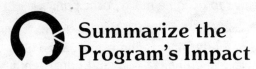

Summarize the Program's Impact

Many programs are minimally effective because participants or leaders — or both — are not clear about the kind of impact they expect the program to have.

There are eight general levels of impact (see page 37) for a workshop or conference — each requiring very different information handling, learning, and planning steps. The first action planning tip is "Know what impact levels you want to achieve."

Obviously, you may have goals at any or all impact levels. Goals for the higher levels (action and results) are likely to — but may not — relate to your pre-program issues.

As one of your final steps before leaving the program, list your goals for each of the eight levels. Be very selective here. This list can be your summary for the entire program and will help you identify the change areas that require more in-depth planning.

Note that the highest results you can achieve at the end of a program are at the "Specific Goals" level (Level 6). This means that goals are as close as you can get to "Action" and "Results" during the program itself. Planning Tips 2 and 3 focus on how you can refine your goals and prepare for action and accomplishment after the program.

Do a Change Analysis

Changing what you actually do (a Level 7 impact) and accomplish (a Level 8 impact) after a program involves more than just intending to do or accomplish something new (Level 6). This is so because changes of these magnitudes are always "system changes" — that is, they have ripple effects on other people (who may have to think, react, or act differently in response to your changes) or on yourself (changing behavior may require new internal dialogue, new uses of information, different relationships with people, new competencies).

If Level 7 and 8 impacts are your goal, then it is important to plan a change strategy for assuring that they occur. This, in turn, requires that you analyze the changes you expect to make.

The answers to three questions can help you do

Action Planning

You can only achieve these levels after the program.

LEVEL 8 RESULTS
What you do produces something important for yourself, others or an organization.

LEVEL 7 ACTION
You do something different — and do it consistently.

You can achieve these results during the program.

LEVEL 6 SPECIFIC GOALS
You set clear goals regarding what to do after the program.

LEVEL 5 CREATIVITY
You develop some new ideas, approaches or theories.

LEVEL 4 PRIORITIES
You reallocate your time.

LEVEL 3 SKILL
You are able to do something new or to do something more competently.

LEVEL 2 KNOWLEDGE
You add information to your memory store.

LEVEL 1 POSITIVE REACTION
You enjoy the program and feel positive about at least some of the content.

a change analysis:

- What further competence do you personally need to build?

- What auxiliary actions do you or others need to take?

- What time lag is likely to occur before you'll reach your goals — before you and others affected by change are comfortable with its requirements and effects?

It's this thinking that will help you see what you really need to do after the program in order to make action and accomplishment happen.

 Plan for Application

Finally, decide what you will do to bring about the changes you've chosen. Consider:

- Where will you go for the information and experiences you need in order to further build your own competence?

- Whom will you involve in planning any auxiliary changes? (Hopefully, you began to involve them before the program.)

- How will you keep your (and others') energy and enthusiasm up during the time lag between setting and achieving your goals?

- What will be the first step?

Carefully thinking about yourself, the real pressures on your time and energy, the other people who may be involved, and the situations that will be affected can help you make the transition from program to action — and ultimately to results.

THE MAIN POINT IS

Results from workshops and conferences are — in the last analysis — very personal issues. For, unless you apply high levels of personal energy and skill to these situations, lasting benefits are unlikely to occur. This has always been true, but the advantages of competent participation and learning have never been more obvious than they are today. Just staying current in any field requires us to be aware of increasing amounts of information, master new skills and techniques, constantly reassess our priorities, and frequently tap into our own creativity.

These, in turn, require all of us to develop our competence in information handling, learning, and change management.

Information handling, learning, and change management skills — and the importance of your desire to use them — are what this book has been about. Hopefully, you have expanded your awareness of your own role in workshops and conferences and will use the "Tips" whenever you participate in programs from now on.

Your payoff? . . . Results, and the high levels of personal satisfaction that come from planning and managing your own learning and change.

"Our Age of Anxiety is, in great part, the result of trying to do today's job with yesterday's tools — with yesterday's concepts." — Marshall McLuhan

ACTION SUMMARY

What do you want to remember from this chapter (in seven or less points)?

_____

_____

_____

_____

_____

_____

_____

What tips will you use (or modify and use)?

_____

_____

_____

_____

_____

_____

NOTE-TAKING

TIPS

Outlines
Indented Notes
Lists
Note Diagrams

Notes can help you:

- clarify

- select key ideas

- organize

- concisely store information.

Notes are an external memory system that can add to your capacity to process information.

It's helpful to know and be able to use several kinds of note systems, because:

Learning and information handling situations differ:

- in how organized or disorganized the data is

- in presentation speed

- in density of facts per time unit.

Your needs vary from situation to situation:

- you may want to remember most of the information — or only a part

- you may want to organize the data — or just jot miscellaneous notes

- you may want to focus on the information itself — or you may want to go beyond it and record potential new behaviors, values, or creative thoughts that occur to you as you handle the information.

There are many kinds of notes that can help you process information. If your notes always look the same, they may not be as effective an information management tool as they could be, for, since situations and your needs vary, notes should vary, too.

This special section will review four note-taking methods that can help you organize and manage information in the variety of program situations you will face in the future. Three are especially useful when information (from a presentation, discussion, etc.) is organized and you want to reproduce that flow of ideas in your notes. These three methods are:

- OUTLINES

- INDENTED NOTES

- LISTS

The fourth note-taking method is useful when you want to organize disorganized data.

- NOTE DIAGRAMS

 # Outlines

Outlines are an excellent method when the information is well organized and you want to reproduce that organization.

GETTING RESULTS THROUGH LEARNING: TIPS FOR PARTICIPANTS IN WORKSHOPS AND CONFERENCES

I. Planning for Results
   A. Preview Program Content and Resources
      1. Review program announcement
      2. Scan list of speakers and participants
   B. Write out Potential Benefits and Applications
      1. Identify current critical issues, problems, concerns
      2. Determine topics to remember
II. Handling Program Materials and Information
   A. Concentrate and Manage Your Motivation
      1. Tips for handling material that is not immediately useful or interesting
         a. Skip the section
         b. Increase overt participation

Getting Rest

43

Indented Notes

This note form does not use alpha-numerics, but does use the visual cueing (indenting) of outlines. At a glance you can distinguish global points from details. Like outlines, indented notes are useful in organized situations.

LEARNING
  Introduction

  - Information processing is not learning

  - Learning strategies are required

  - There are four learning results (memory, skills, values, creativity)

  Tips for Remembering

  - Select

  - Organize

  - Associate

  - Translate

  - Review

  Tips for Skills Development

  - Identify skill steps

  - Etc.

 ## Lists

Lists are also useful in organized situations, especially when your intention is to pull one topic from the many that are presented and quickly record the key implications for you. Lists are usually brief and are intended to be memory joggers rather than detailed reproductions of the material they are based on.

TIPS FOR PRIORITIES

Examination and Change

1. Recognize when priorities are the critical learning issue

2. Compare priorities

3. Examine the pros and cons of priority change

4. Decide priority shifts

5. Develop a payoff list

 ## Note Diagrams
An Organized Solution to Disorganized Information

Outlines, lists and indented notes are linear note systems that assume an organized information presentation. Some lectures and written materials are well organized and can be handled by these note methods.

But what can you do to record — in an organized manner — data that is not well-organized?

YOU CAN USE NOTE DIAGRAMS

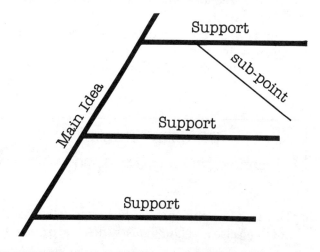

As a backdrop to Note Diagrams, let's take a closer look at what often happens to outlines, indented notes, and lists in workshops and conferences.

A FAMILIAR SCENE

Imagine yourself at a conference session entitled "Industry Trends." The speaker begins his presentation by listing what he intends to talk about: *I'm going to summarize what our research has shown: 1) the technology changes that will occur in the industry by 1990, 2) the external forces that will affect our direction, and 3) the new product lines that are likely to evolve."*

Sounds well organized. You decide to take complete notes and to take these comments back to others in the office. You set up your first outline point . . .

INDUSTRY TRENDS

I. Technology Changes by 1990

But wait . . . the speaker begins to talk about something else . . . *"Our industry has had a unique past. Let's quickly look at where we've been . . ."*

You've just been thrown a curve! Well, . . .

INDUSTRY TRENDS

I. Industry History
  A. 1900 . . .
  B. 1925 . . .
  C. 1950 . . .

Then, the original plan resumes . . .

  D. 1980
II. Technology Changes by 1990
  A. Electronic . . .

Until . .

" . . . actually, what we are seeing in 1990 and beyond had its roots in the 1950's situation I discussed earlier. Let's take a closer look at what happened back then . . ."

Now what do you do? There's no room to add to the 1950's section on your outline. Yet that's where you'd like to put the information about the 1950's.

I. Industry History

    A. 1900 . . .

    B. 1925 . . .

    C. 1950 . . .

    D. 1980 . . .

See next page

II. Technology Changes by 1990

    A. Electronic . . .

Technology Changes in 1990

New Products

External Forces

And, when new main topics emerge, you can add them like this.

Well. The point should be clear. Outlines are often not flexible enough to help you really organize information in workshops and conferences (and in other situations).

On the other hand, note diagrams can help you organize disorganized information and add extra topics without disturbing the idea flow of your notes.

Here's how Note Diagrams could work in the case situation described:

First, after the speaker's opening summary, you could "set up" for the main topics.

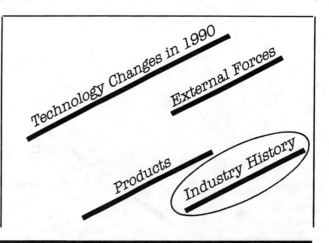

Technology Changes in 1990

External Forces

Products

Industry History

Then, when additional material is introduced, you can expand your notes, either by adding details to points you have already recorded or by adding a whole category labeled "miscellaneous comments."

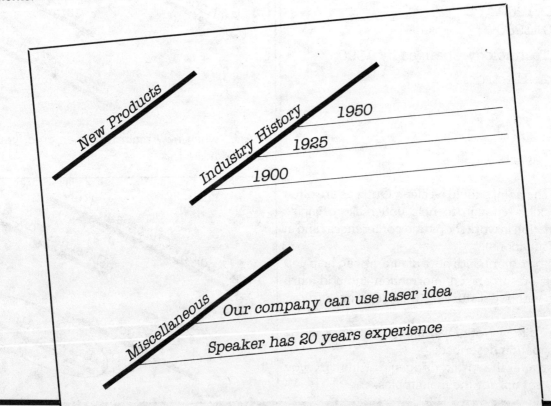

And none of this interferes with your building on the speaker's initial outline:

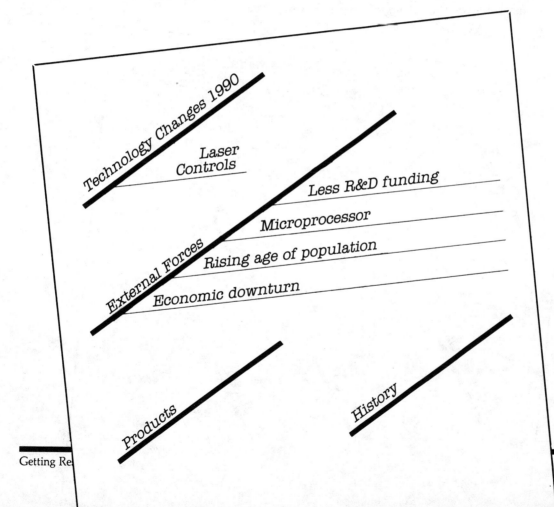

Note diagrams are also a useful reading aid. You can overview the main points of the report, article, or chapter and place the main ideas on diagrams:

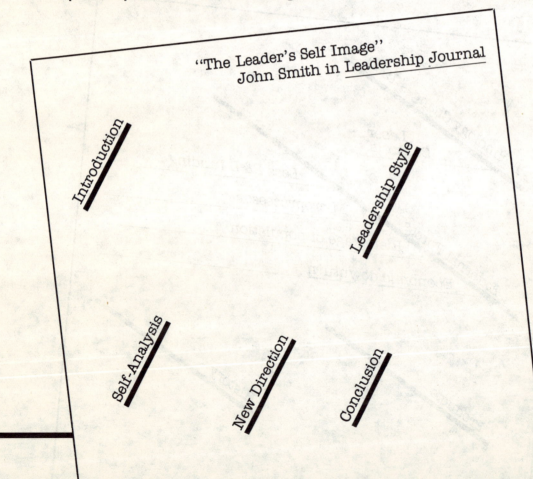

"The Leader's Self Image"
John Smith in Leadership Journal

Introduction

Leadership Style

Self-Analysis

New Direction

Conclusion

Taking

Then you can read the section of materials in any order you want, take notes after each section, and end your reading session with a set of notes that corresponds with the author's organization.

If you have chosen to SKIP any section, your notes will tell you that fact. (You won't have completed that section of the diagram.)

For example:

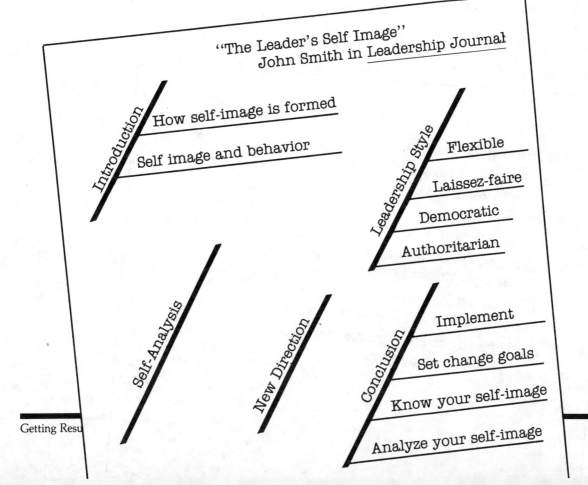

"The Leader's Self Image"
John Smith in Leadership Journal

Introduction
How self-image is formed
Self image and behavior

Leadership Style
Flexible
Laissez-faire
Democratic
Authoritarian

Self-Analysis

New Direction

Conclusion
Implement
Set change goals
Know your self-image
Analyze your self-image

When you review these notes later:
- you'll know at a glance what the key points were
- you'll be able to then review details you've recorded
- you'll know what you decided to skip — and may now choose to read those sections.

The point is, Note Diagrams add new dimensions to note-taking — in workshops, conferences, and in reading — even when they are combined with other note forms:

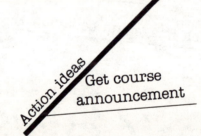

I. Planning for Results
  A. Preview Program Content and Resources
    1. Review program announcement
    2. Scan list of speakers and participants
  B. Write out Potential Benefits and Applications
    1. Identify current critical issues, problems, concerns

Action ideas
Get course announcement

They can help you:

- set up main points — early
- fill in details as they come up
- add and expand categories.

They also help you concentrate and manage bias — for they enable you to:

- focus on main ideas
- link details to the main points that organize them (good both for information processing and remembering)
- get many notes on a page (the fewer pages of notes you take, the less formidable they will look for review)
- use your eyes as an information management aid (Note Diagrams visually map idea relationships)
- take brief, key word notes
- be creative and active as you handle information.

THE MAIN POINT IS

Note-taking can be a powerful information management tool — for listening, reading, and other program (and non-program-related) learning events if you . . .

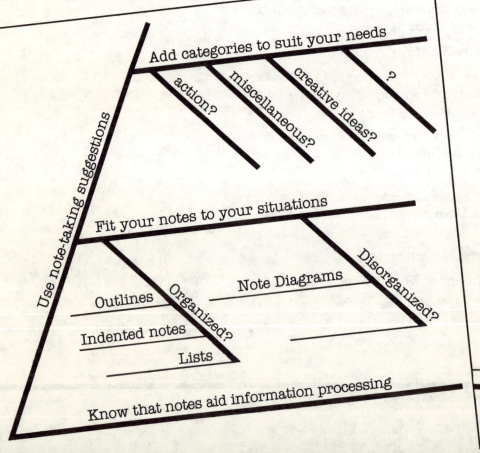

Use note-taking suggestions

Add categories to suit your needs

action?   miscellaneous?   creative ideas?   ?

Fit your notes to your situations

Outlines   Organized?   Note Diagrams   Disorganized?

Indented notes

Lists

Know that notes aid information processing

ACTION SUMMARY

Try using note diagrams to summarize your thoughts from this section.

STRATEGY SUGGESTIONS

Effective information handling requires different strategies for different situations. The "tips" below can help you be more effective in the most commonly occurring workshop and conference situations.

- articles
- books
- case studies
- computer aided learning
- discussions
- film, TV, movies
- lectures
- role plays
- videotape

Strategies for Articles

Benefits
You can read them at your own speed, in your own order and depth. They are portable, personal. You can stop for notes and creative idea recording.

Potential Problems
For many people reading is passive. Needed data may be buried.

TIPS
Overview each article before you read (see first and last paragraphs, bold face type). Overviewing main ideas first sets up the mental filing system for storing and remembering details later.

Write main points down before reading really important articles.

Select and read those parts that relate to your key issues. Skip the rest.

Quickly and flexibly (at varying rates) read, skim, scan, and mark key spots.

Mentally recap or jot down key ideas.

Recognize and manage concentration problems and biases immediately (see Chapter Two).

Strategies for Books

Benefits

You can be highly flexible, varying your own speed, order of chapter coverage, reading depth. (You can skim parts, skip parts, read others in detail.) You can use the index (in the back of the book) to help you quickly find information that relates to topics that interest you. (Researching from key words in the index resembles the approaches we will be using more often in the future as computer data searches — which require us to use key words — become more accessible and useful.)

Potential Problems

Guilt feelings about skipping around in a book may keep you from tapping all the information that could be tapped by selectively reading.

TIPS

Analyze your book before you read, examine your options, and set your goals.

Flip through it, noting how long it is, how many sections it has, the copyright date, what's at the back (Index? Bibliography? Notes? A summary? A section about the author?).

Scan the Index and check off subjects that are important to you. If most of these subjects are treated on discontinuous pages, don't read by chapters — research the pages listed in the index. If there are not many subjects in the index that are relevant to your needs, get another book.

Carefully read the Table of Contents and then mark off two chapters: 1) the chapter where you are likely to find the "key information" or the summary, and 2) the chapter that looks most "interesting" to you. You'll want to read the "interesting chapter" first if you are generally unmotivated, and the "key chapter" first if you're feeling work-oriented.

Determine your plan.

How will this book help you achieve your program purpose(s)?

Will you read from the Index, or by chapter?

Will you take notes? What kinds? On paper or note cards? (Note cards force brevity and can be stored in a file box or in your book.)

How much time will you allow?

Where will you start (in the key or most interesting chapters)?

Skim (read first sentences of paragraphs), *scan* (for reference to specific events, people, etc., that are not necessarily the main points), *select, read, skip,* as you see fit.

Periodically recap — mentally or in note form — in terms of:

- new knowledge to remember
- new behaviors to try
- new values that are emerging — in you
- creative ideas.

Remember that your goals are important in book reading (and all other learning) and that it is perfectly *legitimate* — and actually necessary in these information-overload times — to skip data that is not related to your purpose.

Detect your and the author's values and biases (they'll partly determine what the writer says and how he or she says it, as well as what you will pay attention to).

- separate facts from opinions
- identify assumptions (yours and the author's)
- recognize "propaganda"

 # Strategies for Case Studies

Benefits

They give you practice in problem solving and theory application, help you understand concepts through the study and discussion of concrete situations, and let you experiment with new ideas in a low risk situation.

Potential Problems

The lessons you examine may not be clearly relevant to your own situation — and frequently the case summary and debriefing either do *not occur or are not well-handled by the group leader.*

TIPS

Use efficient reading techniques as you read the case. (Flip through and overview the main ideas before reading details.)

Clearly state the problem and the underlying issues before trying to solve it. Be clear about what are important and unimportant aspects of the case.

Watch your own and others' biases, values, and fixed ways of thinking. Bring values and attitudes out into the open.

Justify your solutions in terms of the key principles the case is supposed to help you explore.

Debrief the case for yourself. (What did you learn that you hope to remember and apply in your real-life situation? What new viewpoints did you examine? What creative ideas occurred to you?) Debriefing in this way will help your learning transfer beyond the case itself.

Strategies for Computer Aided Learning

Benefits

Computers can aid learning in many ways:

- Calculating: You can use the computer as a calculator.

- Inquiry: You can use it to search for information.

- Tutorial: Here, the computer presents concepts, procedures or rules, asks questions, processes answers, and provides right/wrong information.

- Drill & Practice: You can use the computer to practice and test skills.

- Simulation: You can work with the computer in a complex problem solving situation. You receive instant feedback about the impact of your decisions and can test your knowledge in a safe environment without worrying about negative effects. (E.g., a 747 pilot can practice a variety of maneuvers in a simulator without fear of real consequences. A marketing specialist can vary advertising strategies without concern about real market failure.)

- Modeling: Here you can not only practice problem solving, but also build the model itself.

- Instructional Games: You can compete with others, yourself, or the computer to test your knowledge and skills.

- The computer is infinitely patient and is a neutral teacher.

Potential Problems

Computer applications are only as good as the models on which they are based (garbage in, garbage out). Also, unless you are aware of the learning techniques you can use, you may not fully use the system's capabilities.

TIPS

Spend some time learning what the system can do and how to run it.

Find out what provisions have been made to protect your privacy.

Identify the "instructional mode" you are using (calculating, inquiry, tutorial, drill and practice, simulation, modeling, instructional games).

Unless there are time limits, *deliberately make mistakes.* This can bring additional information to the screen (you usually get useful feedback when you enter a wrong answer) or can enable you to practice very subtle predictions (e.g., "If I make this adjustment in the formula, the rocket should miss the moon by one million miles . . . oops . . . I miscalculated").

 # Strategies for Discussions

Benefits

Discussions enable you to clarify ideas. They stimulate interest, attention, discovery, and creativity. They encourage you to examine ideas in your own words (making it easier to remember) and to clarify your own assumptions and values. You can check out ideas with others.

Potential Problems

Discussions require listening and group interaction skills. Group norms may discourage real issue discussion. Values and biases may not be brought into the open where they can be dealt with.

TIPS

Have a dual goal of both sharing and learning.

Be aware of similarities and differences in biases. Lay them on the table as you do facts.

Recognize that *the purpose of many discussions is idea exploration,* not agreement. Clarify which purpose is involved.

Summarize periodically to check your perception of what is happening. Restating others' viewpoints can also help you see the vulnerable side of your own view — and is a good values clarification technique.

If your interest is waning — *pair up with someone* who is enthusiastic.

Help make the Group Process effective:

Play a variety of "task-related roles":

- initiate ideas
- give and seek out information and opinions

- synthesize and summarize
- clarify and test consensus.

Play a variety of "people centered roles":

- empathize — try to understand where others are coming from
- compromise, where appropriate
- help keep communication channels open
- support other people's contributions.

 # Strategies for Film, TV, Movies

Benefits

These can be a vivid way to learn how specific actions work in close-to-real-life situations. They are usually easy to concentrate on because of their pace and sight/sound impact.

Potential Problems

You won't realize the full benefit of film, TV, movies, unless you deliberately examine their purposes and lessons.

TIPS

Know beforehand, if possible, what the key points will be, and be alert for examples as you watch.

Know and act on the fact that *there is more to most stories* than just the story itself. Often there is:

- a lesson(s)
- some historical significance, either direct (as in an historical drama), or indirect (as in a show or story that portrays the values and behaviors of a group or class)
- opportunity for vicarious experience (film and TV invite emotional involvement that can be as valuable and have as much impact as many personal experiences do).

Use the above knowledge in two ways:

- to help you direct your attention as you're watching (to the lesson, the historical significance, the vicarious experiences involved)
- to help you summarize your learnings at the end.

Unless you summarize — mentally, through discussion or on paper — you risk losing a great deal of learning.

 # Strategies for Lectures

Benefits

Lectures can be a short cut into information when

the speaker is a specialist and is current in his/her field.

Potential Problems

Presentations encourage listeners to be passive.

TIPS

Listen for main ideas and key terms at the outset and throughout the talk. This will give you a mental set for the information and help you recognize relevant details as you listen.

Use notes to help you:

- zero in on main ideas and key terms

- keep yourself interested and active

- organize the material. (Use outlines for an organized lecture, note diagrams for a disorganized lecture that you want to organize, jots for miscellaneous notes, a tape recorder for difficult, detailed, fast-paced important material.)

Determine the speaker's values by asking:

- What points does he/she emphasize?

- What facts are left out?

- How emotional is the language?

- What other points of view are possible?

Mentally recap key points and, if possible, discuss them soon after. This can greatly aid retention.

Use as much of the lecturer's expertise as you can — ASK — what are the best information sources in this field (writers, subject specialists, periodicals, abstracts and computer searches, libraries, associations)?

 # Strategies for Role Plays

Benefits

Role plays can help you examine issues, situations, and actions from other perspectives, and they enable you to test new ideas, actions, feelings, and reactions in a low risk activity.

Potential Problems

It is difficult to stay in a role. And, without a role play debriefing, lessons may not be clear.

TIPS

Be clear about the:

- purposes

- problem or issue

- its potential relevance to you

- where action is supposed to take place

- the general characteristics of the character you are playing

- the knowledge, skills, and values required by the role.

Try to *stay in your role.*

Try to play a role you can learn from (e.g., one that represents a different point of view from your own).

Watch and mentally note reactions of other participants. These may be the basis for deciding whether or not to apply what you tried in the role play.

If you are part of the audience, know

- what to look for

- whom you will identify with.

Debrief — summarize your learnings after the acting ends.

Be supportive of others in their "dramatic" efforts.

Strategies for Videotape

Benefits

You can see yourself "as others see you," and can stop and rerun the action.

Potential Problems

It's tempting to treat a video replay like TV — to watch uncritically and for entertainment. Many of us are not astute observers of behavior — and may miss key actions as we watch the replays.

TIPS

Before taping, have a clear understanding of the situations and roles you are supposed to play.

Have one or two specific behaviors or skills you will try to do and one or two you will try not to do as you tape. Intend to critique yourself later mainly regarding these few key points. Don't try to do and look for everything.

As you watch the playback, *try to observe and analyze the behaviors.* Resist the temptation to be a passive spectator.

Discuss your observation by describing (not judging) the behaviors you observe in others and yourself, and by asking others' reactions to the new behaviors you tried.

Summarize what you have learned about yourself and describe one or two behavior, knowledge, or value changes you want to implement.

THE MAIN POINT IS

The strategies you use can have major effects on your information processing and learning effectiveness. Vary what you do based on your needs and on the special requirements of the methods and media you face. Learning will be more interesting and you'll more likely reap benefits if you manage your information processing this way.

BIBLIOGRAPHY

Anderson, B. *Cognitive Psychology*. New York: Academic Press, 1975.

Bandura, A. *Principles of Behavior Modification*. New York: Holt, Rinehart & Winston, 1969.

Bandt, P., Meara, N., & Schmidt, L. *A Time to Learn*. New York: Holt, Rinehart & Winston, 1974.

Barnett, H.G. *Innovation: The Basis of Cultural Change*. New York: McGraw-Hill, 1953.

Bennis, W., Benne, K., Chin, R. & Corey, R. *The Planning of Change* (3rd ed.). New York: Holt, Rinehart & Winston, 1976.

Biondi, A. *Have an Affair with Your Mind*. Great Neck, N.Y.: Creative Synergetic Assoc., 1974.

deBono, E. *Mechanisms of Mind*. New York: Basic Books, Inc., 1969.

Carkhuff, R.R. *Helping and Human Relations, A Primer for Lay and Professional Helpers (Vol II, Practice and Research)*. New York: Holt, Rinehart & Winston, 1969.

Davis, G.B. *Management Information Systems: Conceptual Foundation, Structure, and Development*. New York: McGraw-Hill, 1974.

Dill, W., Crowston, W. & Elton, E. Strategies for Self-Education. *Harvard Business Review,* Nov. Dec., 1965.

Ellis, A. & Harper, R. *A Guide to Rational Living*. Hollywood, Calif.: Wilshire Book Co., 1961.

Faure, E. *Learning to Be, The World of Education Today and Tomorrow*. Paris, France: UNESCO, 1972.

Fishbein, M. & Ajzen, I. *Belief, Attitude, Intention and Behavior*. Reading, Mass.: Addison-Wesley, 1975.

Havelock, R. & Havelock, M. *Training for Change Agents*. Ann Arbor, Mich.: Institute for Social Research, University of Michigan, 1973.

Hill, W. *Learning: A Survey of Psychological Interpretations*. Scranton, Penn.: Chandler Publishing Co., 1971.

Howe, M. *Adult Learning: Psychological and Research Applications*. Chichester, Eng.: John Wiley & Sons, 1977.

Jahoda, M. *Attitudes*. Baltimore: Penguin Books, 1966.

Knowles, M. *Self-Directed Learning*. New York: Association Press, 1975.

Knowles, M. *The Modern Practice of Adult Education*. New York: Association Press, 1970.

Laird, D. *Approaches to Training and Development*. Reading, Mass.: Addison-Wesley, 1978.

Laszlo, E. Systems Philosophy of Human Values, *Behavioral Science,* July 1973, *18*(4).

Lorayne, H. & Lucas, J. *The Memory Book*. New York: Ballantine Books, 1974.

Mahoney, M. & Thoresen, C. *Self-Control: Power to the Person*. Monterey, Calif.: Brooks/Cole, 1974.

McKeachie, W. *Teaching Tips*. Lexington, Mass.: D.C. Heath & Co., 1969.

McLagan, P. Competency Models, *Training and Development Journal,* December, 1980.

McLagan, P. Computer Aided Instruction, *Training Magazine,* Sept. 1977.

McLagan, P. *Helping Others Learn: Designing Programs for Adults*. Reading, Mass.: Addison-Wesley, 1978.

McLuhan, M. *Understanding Media: The Extensions of Man.* New York: New American Library, 1964.

Meichenbaum, D. *Cognitive Behavior Modification, An Integrative Approach.* New York: Plenum Press, 1977.

Miller, G. The Magical Number Seven, Plus or Minus Two: Some Limits on Our Capability for Processing Information, *Psychological Review,* Mar. 1956, *63*(2), 81-97.

Miller, G., Galanter, E., & Pribram, K. *Plans and the Structure of Behavior.* New York: Holt, Rinehart & Winston, 1960.

Newell, A. & Simon, H. *Human Problem Solving.* Engelwood Cliffs, N.J.: Prentice Hall, Inc., 1972.

Norman, D. *Memory and Attention: An Introduction to Human Information Processing.* New York: John Wiley & Sons, 1969.

Postman L. & Keppel, G. (Eds.). *Verbal Learning and Memory.* Baltimore: Penguin Books, 1969.

Rogers, C.R. *Freedom to Learn.* Columbus, Ohio: Charles Merrill Publishing, 1969.

Rokeach, M. *The Nature of Human Values.* New York: Free Press, 1973.

Tough, A. *The Adult's Learning Projects.* Austin, Tex.: Learning Concepts, 1971.

Wason, P. & Johnson-Laird, P. (Eds.). *Thinking and Reasoning.* Baltimore: Penguin Books, 1968.

Weinland, J. *How to Improve Your Memory.* New York: Barnes & Noble, 1957.

Williams, R. & Long, I. *Toward a Self-Managed Life Style.* Boston: Houghton-Mifflin Co., 1975.

Winters, Kolb, & Griffith. Capacity for Self-Direction, *Journal of Consulting and Clinical Psychology,* 1968, *32*(1), 35-41.

Wirsing, M. *Teaching and Philosophy: A Synthesis.* New York: Houghton-Mifflin Co., 1972.

ABOUT THE AUTHOR

"There are two major ways we can help people learn and manage information more effectively," says Pat McLagan, who has been concerned about how adults learn and manage information since her Phi Beta Kappa years as a student at the University of Minnesota. "Educators, writers, training and development specialists, meeting planners, speakers can present information more effectively. But adults — all of us — must also use and continue to develop better learning and information management methods."

Pat, who holds an MA in Adult Education from the University of Minnesota, taught learning skills there until becoming president of McLagan & Associates, Inc. She has helped managers, learners, educators and conference planners focus on "getting results." She and her colleagues have worked with a broad range of organizations and associations including NASA, General Electric, Honeywell, Citibank, General Mills, Chase Manhattan Bank, Tektronix and the American Society of Association Executives to help address a broad range of human resource development issues — including conference and program design, and management and professional development.

She has authored many books and articles, including *Helping Others Learn: Designing Programs for Adults* (Addison-Wesley, 1978); "Computer-Aided Instruction," *Training Magazine*, 1977; "Competency Models," *ASTD Training and Development Journal*, 1980; *Learning to Learn*, a Control Data *Plato* program; and *On The Level: Tips to Help Managers and Employees Communicate About Performance* (McLagan & Associates Products, Inc., 1982); "Models for Excellence: The Results of the ASTD Training and Development Competency Study," *ASTD Training and Development Journal*, 1983; and *Models For Excellence: The Conclusions and Recommendations of the ASTD Training and Development Competency Study* (ASTD Press, 1983).

An internationally known speaker on adult learning, management and professional development, design, competency modeling, and career and organization development issues, she has held leadership positions in the American Society for Training and Development (ASTD) and the Minneapolis United Way.